HISTORY OF HURRICANES

TERESA CADER

HISTORY OF HURRICANES

poems

TRIQUARTERLY BOOKS
NORTHWESTERN UNIVERSITY PRESS
EVANSTON, ILLINOIS

TriQuarterly Books
Northwestern University Press
www.nupress.northwestern.edu

Printed in the United States of America

10   9   8   7   6   5   4   3   2   1

Library of Congress Cataloging-in-Publication Data

Cader, Teresa.
     History of hurricanes : poems / Teresa Cader.
        p. cm.
     Includes bibliographical references.
        ISBN 978-0-8101-2575-9 (cloth : alk. paper)—
     ISBN 978-0-8101-2576-6 (pbk. : alk. paper)
        I. Title.
     PS3553.A3134H57 2009
     811.54—dc22

                                              2008048240

For Jerry, Katherine, and Emma

The sun, which has all those planets revolving around it and dependent on it for orderly function, can ripen a bunch of grapes as though it had nothing else to do.

Galileo

CONTENTS

ACKNOWLEDGMENTS

I am grateful to the editors of the following publications in which these poems first appeared:

AGNI: "History of Hurricanes," "The New Creation," "Pure Music"

The Atlantic Monthly: "Aria"

Bat City Review: "Oasis"

Caribbean Writing Today: "Glimpse—mid-morning"

Crab Orchard Review: "Kraków Blues"

FIELD: "Counterpoint"

Harvard Review: "Blue Table with Pomegranates," "Elsewhere"

MIT Faculty Newsletter: "Slave Huts, Bonaire," "Summer without Summering"

Perihelion: " 'Dwell Nowhere and Bring Forth the Mind,' " "The Raymond-Harrington House, 1872"

Poetry: "Anywhere," "Boneshaker," "Spoilers"

Seneca Review: "Habits," "Nowhere"

Slate: "A Bristle of Wings in the Ivy," "First Laws," "Indwelling," "Petrified Light," and "September 11" (in "Poetry and September 11: A Guided Anthology," edited by Robert Pinsky)

Southern Poetry Review: "Spoon, Fork, Plate"

Southwest Review: "Burying Ground"

"September 11" has been reprinted in *Conversation Pieces: Poems That Talk to Other Poems,* edited by Kurt Brown and Harold Schechter (New York: Everyman's Library Pocket Poets, Alfred A. Knopf, 2007). It has also been included in the global online art archive The Legacy Project.

HISTORY OF HURRICANES

History of Hurricanes

Because we cannot know—

we plant crops, make love in the light of our not-knowing

A Minuteman prods cows from the Green with his musket,
his waxed paper windows snapping in the wind,
stiletto stalks in the herb garden upright—Now

blown sideways—Now weighted down in genuflection,

not toward,

And a frail man holding an Imari teacup paces at daybreak
       in his courtyard in Kyoto

a cherry tree petaling the stones pink and slippery
       in the weeks he lay feverish

waiting for word from the doctor, checking for signs—Now

in the season of earthenware sturdiness and dependency
       it must begin, the season of his recovery

       ~

No whirling dervish on the radar, no radar, no brackets
no voices warning—no Voice—fugue of trees, lightning

Because we cannot know, we imagine

What will happen to me without you?

       ~

I know some things I remember—

the Delaware River two stories high inside the brick houses
cars floating past Trenton like a regiment on display
brown water climbing our basement stairs two at a time

~

Like months of remission—
                         the eye shifts

the waxed paper windows
                         burst behind the flapping shutters—

and how could he save his child after that calm,
a man who'd never seen a roof sheared off?

~

Across town the ninth graders in their cutoffs:
Science sucks, they grouse. *Stupid history of hurricanes.*

No one can remember one;

velocity, storm surge—
                         abstractions
the earth churns as Isabel rips through Buzzard's Bay

A hurricane, as one meaning has it:
a large crowded assembly of fashionable people at a private house

~

The river cannot remember its flooding—

      I worry you will forget to check
           the watermarks in time

An echo of feet on stone is all the neighbors
      knew of their neighbor,
           a lover of cherry trees

and of his wife who prayed for him at the shrine,
her hair swept up in his favorite onyx comb

Boneshaker

Not to need a horse, or have to wait for a carriage,
To slip away, jut away, pedal off

On a whim or in a fury, without permission or charge,
With nothing but wind and pebbles,

Cumulus dust or a heckle of driven rain,
In knickers or barn bibs—and one day, bloomers—

Out of the sweltering clan, fetid farmhouse,
Loose on a lane of poplars upright as gendarmes,

Churning rutted roads speckled with poppies,
Grazed by pheasant or hare,

Into night, if need be, or dawn's lavender light
Before anyone checks the beds,

Out of the argument, or the sermon,
To the spokes and wheels, the steering bar and column,

The wooden seat searing the tailbone,
The spinal S a serpentine lash

In a field of raspberries unglimpsed from trains,
Something idiosyncratic, shaped by will

And fueled by muscle, a boneshaker
Taking its rider away—there!—or anywhere.

Anywhere

"Whither goes the soul when the body dies?" the Scholar asks the Master,
and my daughter wanted to know how to send the goldfish bowl to heaven

with the three goldfish we buried under the rose of Sharon. The Scholar
sits cross-legged on the floor, waits with humility for a sign.

My daughter listened to her friend's mother conduct a funeral for a mouse:
"She was a hundred and three by human standards. She lived a good life."

"What's a good life?" my daughter wanted to know, as we stood in line
at Burger King. The Master replies, "There is no necessity for it

to go anywhere." The Scholar sips plum blossom tea alone in his room.
"For this, I have wasted my youth, abandoned my family," he writes

in his book of questions. "For this my eyes have been blinded."
"When I die me," my daughter announced at bedtime, "I want Babar

to come, too. Why did the mouse have to die alone?" The Scholar waits
for the Master by the door of the temple, but it is cold and raining

and the Master is at home, old and coughing in his bed.
"Whither shall I go now to search?" the Scholar asks the wet leaves.

"Anywhere" they answer in delicate tones. "But there is no necessity
to go anywhere." "Could we say a prayer for the mouse?" my daughter

asked when I turned out her light. "Of course," I said: *A mouse
is miracle enough to stagger sextillions of infidels* into sleep.

Nowhere

I go nowhere on purpose; I happen by.
I do not search for you; I watch.
Why have you forgotten me?
Why do the stone walls shudder as I approach?

I do not search for you, I watch,
Knowing I cannot will you to come.
Why do the stone walls shudder? As I approach,
Crocuses bluster into clumps of sod.

Knowing I cannot will you to come,
I observe ruts where I snowshoed in March.
Crocuses bluster into clumps of sod:
I don't reproach the spring for starting up again.

The ruts where I snowshoed in March
Remind me the sun will not wait.
I don't reproach the spring for starting up again;
I want to be done with winter.

Remind me the sun won't wait—
In the phlox and lichen in the stone walls.
I want to be done with winter.
The sealed spaces must be forced apart.

In the phlox and lichen in the stone walls,
Show me a rift, a place for summer blossoms.
The sealed spaces must be forced apart
So the wall can be repaired, rebalanced.

Show me a rift, a place for summer blossoms
After months of dead vines, crusted mud.
The wall could be repaired, rebalanced
In time to pick clean what has silenced me.

After months of dead vines, crusted mud,
You might find me interesting, might show yourself
In time to pick clean what has silenced me.
I watch a rotten leaf dried by the sun.

You *might* find me interesting, *might* show yourself—
I despise this waiting, this uncertainty.
I watch a rotten leaf dried by the sun:
I am this waiting and this watching.

Why have you forgotten me?
I go nowhere on purpose; I happen by.

Spoilers

I like weeding the garden. I like rooting out the spoilers. I must be old.
The symmetry of Asiatic lilies pleases me. Elephant Ears look sloppy.

I like figuring out which friends are loyal and counting them on lists.
I eat less for dinner. The beach holds fewer charms. I am afraid of sun.

My children are young. Already I can't tolerate their music. They talk back
in ways unheard of in my time. Will I sleep better in an empty nest

and therefore be more civil? A double feature is impossible, a double bed
too small. A double life seems less immoral than exhausting.

I want intimacy and order and beauty. I require passion. Of course I am
difficult to live with. Best to leave me alone and don't overwater.

Maybe I am old but not wise. I am too attached to outcome.
I planted the garden and the children, yes. I tend them like they're mine.

Burying Ground

An arrow marks the path past cars and barns
on Massachusetts Avenue, a craggy cairn

forgotten in the April din of Battle Green
enactments, fife and drums of Revolution.

Six years ago my daughter's third grade class
sketched the trees, unearthed the stilted verse

Abel Webster chiseled into slate, stone
so old the lines are scored with lichen.

The teacher organized a hunt: find a full
moon near *memento mori;* a grinning skull;

colonial tombs of Hancock, Parker, Bowman,
and Clarke, Hastings, Diamond, Harrington,

who gave our streets and schools their names;
the grassy spot where eight Minutemen

were buried April 19 (reburied in a mound
on the Green, the first monument founded

to common soldiers). Find the elegant tomb
of Ebenezer Fisk, his prophecy of doom:

> *Time was I stood as thou dost now*
> *And viewed ye dead as thou dost me*
> *Ere long you lie as low as I*
> *And others stand & gaze at thee.*

His portrait, carved precisely, shows a mass
of squiggled curls, six buttons, and a haughty gaze.

And Bithian Fisk, his plainly dressed dour wife
(she's got no buttons), resigned to death:

 No house of pleasure here above ground
 Do I expect to have;
 My bed of rest for sleeping found,
 I've made the silent grave.

Locate abstracted faces, almond lids
like Picasso's, with rectangular lips,

and angels with swooping arched wings,
eyes closed or open—one cross-eyed—who ring

the tombs of Cutler, Locke, Munroe, and Prentice,
the cherubim of death, sweet and ghoulish.

My daughter found the Childs monument,
not discussed, not on the field trip hunt:

 Erected to the memory of 6 children
 of Mr. Abijah Childs & Mrs. Sarah his wife

She copied the list of ages, not alphabetical,
the dates, all in '78, not chronological:

 Sarah, August 28, Aged 8 months, 11 days
 Eunice, August 23, Aged 12 years, 3 months, 8 days
 Abijah, September 6, Aged 11 years, 37 days
 Abigail, August 29, Aged 7 years, 7 months, 11 days
 Benj~n, August 21, Aged 4 years, 9 months, 8 days
 Moses, August 19, Aged 3 years wanting 8 days

She asked, "What does 'wanting 8 days mean'?"
Eyes wide: "What happened to them?"

War in Lexington. Fear. Near starvation.
In eighteen days the deaths of six children.

Disease. Epidemics. "Could be smallpox," I said.
"Don't worry. It's been eradicated."

She wasn't worried. Summer's rebound
beckoned for another bike ride into town.

But I went back to read the stones more closely.
Thomas Locke, who *died Suddenly:*

> *Watch ye therefore, for ye know not*
> *When ye master of ye houre cometh,*
>
> *of even, or at midnight, or at cock-crowing*
> *or in the morning.*

And noticed "Dead of the Pox" on tombs plain,
or pessimistic, unlike faithful Mary Buckman's:

> *Dear Friends for me pray do not weep*
> *I am not dead but here do sleep*

I skirted a windfall of downed trees—limbs,
the only wood that didn't belong to the King,

communal fuel for a fire at the Buckman Tavern
between Sunday services, where people "put on

the dog" in turns, hoisting the tavern mutt
onto half-frozen foot and sodden boot

to thaw them for the deep freeze afternoon
in the unheated Congregational church on the Green,

listening to Jonas Clarke foment revolution,
equating common good and common men,

while parents like the Childs shushed their brood
in pews where dust motes clung to the wood.

Summer without Summering

1.

Peculiar birdcall. Gray-haired man stops
Daily to scan the sycamore. To listen.
Some sort of fungus on the leaves.
Huge squirrel nest in the crook.
Let someone else name the call, the infestation.
In the garden at the verdigris table,
We eat grilled shrimp, swat late afternoon bees.
An inlet of peace as twilight narrows its gaze.
Faces soften in amber shadow.
What I've wanted might be this.

2.

Damp mists blow inland, the evergreens
In the yard still drip last night's rain. Thunder
Lurks over the neighbor's roof. Wicker chair,
Tea, a book. Upstairs, my child belts "Country
Roads," her first mezzo solo. I listen
On the porch, imagining a stage. There is hope
In the world of ordinary change, the song
Opening her throat like a hollow reed.

3.

On Long Beach Island mosquito sirens spiraled
Around our ears in firelight, squads of June bugs
Zapped our faces when the wind shifts broke
Across the dunes. Blues ran in silver streaks.

My father dug his heels into the shore, surf-fished
Between riptide channels. Night swallowed
Sight, moonless, cold. I sit in the hot tub tonight
Watching stars cascade like fizzled fireworks.
They were God to me on that deserted shore,
A faint display of indifferent light.

4.

We had no pool to swim in, no cabin to rent, no walks
In the forest of Cologne. Mushrooms were our habitat
In Polish Pittsfield, fried straight from the woods, mixed
With seasoned eggs. This summer I'm cooking soups,
Fish in sauce. We grilled scrod on Martha's Vineyard
The summer before my friend killed herself. It fell apart
On the grate, a white hash. I love the riffs of oak leaves
Tonight, wafting in and out of windows. I love the reprieve.

Blue Table with Pomegranates

In Siena in October, the terrace russet with sunset—
   I know how the cobalt blue deepens,

                     The acrid skins
              Crater shadow and soft pulp;

Flourishes yellow as squash burnishing the underbellies—

You core the pomegranates with a paring knife.

              Overripe
By a day, they yield oiled seeds and a scent
                       Of lemon—

I know how your hands smooth skin, stroke hair.
   That much I allow myself to imagine of your body
                     Taken from me someday,

                And the table—

   Already spoken for by a young couple at the iron gate—
     Perfect except for some knife marks and stains.

Winter

I, singularly moved
To love the lovely that are not beloved,
Of all the seasons, most
Love Winter . . .

Coventry Patmore (1823–1895)

1.

The wind as source. Steroid shot in the cuff that won't
rotate. Flip the turn signal? Lift the heavy green-

rimmed plates from the second shelf? Rusty-hinged
bone spur like a jagged root, the untrimmed sycamore

limb that scrapes my window. The accident. Now, wind
eighty miles an hour: the kitchen door's convulsing rip.

Needle threading bone, subclavicle. So the arm can move
upright. Knock on wood meant oak: hit most by lightning,

oak harbored Zeus. In ancient Egypt sycamore trumped oak.
Mine is shedding bark like a machine shredding fact.

I salute them all: those who knock, shred,
thread the needles, force that gusts through our homes,

uproots our daily. The wind in which a scent of linden
calls a reindeer herd across the tundra, thirty below,

the human herd in tents, inventing the wind god. *Let*
my house survive, my arm wave in the air like a wind sock.

2.

Ten Shopping Days Till . . . Days devoted
to Saturn—"Were you here, I would confer with you,"

Seneca the Younger wrote to his friend, "whether to eve
in our usual way, or, to avoid singularity,

both take a better supper and throw off the toga."
Worshippers of the god of seed time had opted for skin.

A festival of disorder: children headed the home, masters
became slaves, and masquerades kept the darkest nights

lit till dawn. The Lord of Misrule was crowned in my kitchen
last year, enthroned on a stool beside the roast duck. Boar-

bellied, red as a poinsettia, he ranted like an also-ran in a stump
speech, finger waving like a teacher's blackboard pointer.

Some year, I'll go to the woods, to a hut near a brook:
moonlight on ice, storm clouds brokering calm absences.

This year suddenly old, you lay your head on the table
like a toddler past nap time. I was tired of shouting into

your deaf ears. Around us, the fruit-stuffed Cornish hens,
salmon mousse, chocolates. On your place card I saw: Dying.

3.

It's not just proximity that creates warmth, or light-infused
afternoons over Mocha Grande. It's angle and degree.

The earth's closest to the sun on December 21. When we're
closest, as in a single bed under a single sheet,

are we eclipsed icons, turned toward each other's sun?
I could answer either way. Dressed in midnight blue satin, black

velvet, I step on your toes as we fox-trot past the ballroom band.
You kiss my neck. The river clogs beneath the boathouse, oblivious

to our yearly demarcation. By eleven, we'll be one sweaty mess
chanting in Mayan for the sun to return. Suppose we hiked into Irish

Newgrange at dawn when winter solstice rays penetrate
the slivered stone at the precise angle of illumination:

spirals, disks, eyes chiseled five thousand years ago
to celebrate the turning. I probe your eyes in candle waver,

see the earth tilting amongst stars and planets.
Angles make orgasms. And arguments. Shadows and tone.

The angle of fingers on the keys. The arthroscopic knife
severing tissue. As the sun is our god, we turn. And then: back.

4.

Monet stood in a field near his house in Giverny
as freezing mist unearthed blue shade from orange

snow-lit haystacks. "I apologize to those in hell
for my disturbances," Robert Bly wrote.

"Reason and despair live in the same house."
Maybe that's why Monet painted outside in winter,

his new portable easel and metal paint tubes in hand,
his house out of sight. Light makes color:

green shadow of a wooden brush. Light keeps the blues
at bay: witness my full-spectrum lamp.

And I believe it when I walk the dog at noon, snowflakes
throwing prisms. Shadows stop hanging like metaphors

under the asphalt roofs. Maybe that's why each haystack
in each moment is untranslatable.

"He taught me art might not be about objects," Duchamp said,
seeing Monet's sequence lined up by hue and nuance.

Where is the farmer whose primal stook weathered winter
in the field and on Monet's canvases? Dead, of course.

I scan my sycamore, hour by hour.

5.

Ice breaker. A good joke. The perfect anecdote. A frip of news off
NPR. Thawed tongues and flushed cheeks. Another "God bless"

in the vodka toast. One of my selves is an *ice maker,* all mannered
bow tie and loathsome game of cricket on manicured lawns.

The Russian icebreaker *Moskva* cut a channel twelve miles long
and seventy yards wide to free a thousand trapped beluga whales.

The whales wouldn't leave—they remembered human
gill nets, sweep nets, seines, Norwegian, Russian, Eskimo butcher ships—

But *Moskva*'s loudspeakers blasted symphonies across the ice.
With barks, squawks, jaw clasps, whistles, squalls, buzzes,

whinnies, and chirps, they sounded like an orchestra tuning up,
and off they went in file behind the ship, led to the open sea

by human mercy and their own echolocation:
I listen for those who think to try the music.

Petrified Light

I studied the tiny insect trapped in amber at the Museum of Science.
Seventy-million-year-old pine resin from the once tropical Baltics,
Petrified into a sarcophagus of honey light. *There you are,* I said.
To the bug, my alter ego. To the amber, my weight of captivity
And stasis. No one heard me mouthing off to the exhibit case.
My daughter watched a series of balls bong their obstacle course,
Plinging bells and tilting pulleys. My husband studied the underbelly
Of a fake lightning bug in the next exhibit. *Amazing,*
He complimented the frog whose belly glowed with glowworms,
And the syncopated sex rhythms of tropical lightning bugs who flash
In unison. So much cellular insight for a Sunday afternoon. Awe
Was the thing I didn't have: hard floors and sore instep, maybe. Awe
Is what the exhibits design for. The three-foot Black Widow caught
My peripheral. *Whoa,* I said to my ordinary. To my stubborn. To fear's
Onion smell welling up in my armpits. What we have here is a body
Created for me. A creature of wild and deadly desire. *Bad.*

Indwelling

In the crazy guest who saws off the chair legs,

In the wind hissing beneath the door sweep,
A tribe of mice squeezing through pocket doors,

In the pants pockets where the evidence remains,
Those filaments of wool in the moth-eaten rug,

In the masquerade of motion that sets off the alarm,
The alarm that arrives via air waves at dinnertime,

In the worm that opens email, eats the address book,
The virus propagating on the unsuspecting screen,

In the cell that missed a loop of timing and purpose,
The unpaid tax surfacing like a submarine,

In the bloody stool and saliva, mucus and membrane,
Slits of sunlight discoloring blue curtains,

In the broken gutter where ice dams pry up the roof,
A crack in the skylight where mold sifts down,

In the contractor hammering windmills on shingles,
The carpenter bees burrowing barracks into the attic,

In the funneling, the grating, the sagging, the gravitating—
O icon of muck and filch, there is nothing you won't

Divide, opening trapdoors we forget to close.

Nocturne

The night racks my bones, O streetlamp,
as you shine temperate through my window.

Your current pulls me briefly past Charybdis;
sucked back to the edge, eddies of pain

spin like pinwheels stripped of their stripes.
The curtain waves its white flag, panes streaked

with dust undulate in luster. (I must be mad
to talk to a streetlamp.) Forced hot water chortles

through baseboard pipes; the bathroom faucet
dribbles its metronome of disrepair.

I despise my skeleton crew of antidotes:
white pill bottles with childproof lids,

therapeutic pillow, nightstand jumbled
with easy reads, comforter fluffed up

like a puffin on an iceberg. Nearby, sleepers
shift their linen sheets, plow dream tides in oblivion,

while I trim ripped sails. Planet of my night, star
rising to steer me out of the whirlpool, by day

you're an oblong eyesore of gray aluminum
dangling from a telephone pole and clumped wires.

Your ugliness and my pain align orbits in sunlight,
barely noticeable if I concentrate on wild asters

and dandelions blooming in the field behind the pole,
or the black Lab lifting its leg like an acrobat—

a mere dim glint in the traffic of vision
and practicality. But by night you are all radiance,

and I seared flesh. You render me visible—to whom
I don't know—my bed lit like a Rembrandt.

The Raymond-Harrington House, 1872

Large enough to shelter four families, tall enough to eclipse the sun
late morning, maker of shadows a shade garden connoisseur would covet,

the new mansion thrusting against our fence, a mix of catamaran
and state prison, has shredded Japanese cherry trees and left a fifteen

foot mud perimeter for a yard. Stone wall, forsythia, giant honeysuckle
Philip Freneau might have immortalized, gone. The Civil War sycamore

is wrapped for another blacktopping of its root system. Thoreau and Emerson,
one town over, would have had one word, *excess.* I dreamed I had gone

to a writers' conference. No one wanted to speak in words, to think about words.
It had become fashionable to push small white beads together on a wooden plate.

Asked my reaction, I could say nothing. I couldn't count fast enough.
Mark Strand walked out of the conference, and others, too. Some loved the codes,

the absence of tonality. I was deafened by hammers and saws,
the Caterpillar jaws spewing asphalt. I tried to sound things out, to capture

the rhythm of spaces. The unsayable is always being said in one way
or another. One needs a permit to build, a license. One needs a variance

to destroy what has already been built. But even words do not capture the *my*
in "my light will be destroyed" because the *my* is not mine.

Jonathan Harrington fought April 19 on the Lexington Green and died
on his doorstep. No one talked much in that battle. Raymond owned

the land on this street where the work crews start pounding at dawn.
Nothing can be said to stop it. Beads of sweat glisten on new panes.

Glimpse—mid-morning

Amherst

What was the secret—a mad simplicity—
myopia—sunlight on wide floorboards
not besmirched by congress or convocation—

honey and alabaster—furtive or bold
as a glance from the bedroom door—

a chosen silence—mote
of distilled listening—a bluebird jangling
nerves into ecstatic isolation—

framed view of hemlocks
rendered skeletal—

What was the passion—an architecture
imposed on unclaimed space—
a stay against execution—

Why did her room—on the flat world's
edge—a heresy—
send galleons to eternity—

The soul selecting temporal
handmaidens—material midwives—

My gaze on the doorsill—fleeting shadow—
attentive to the chamber pot
by her bed—rim roiled in August humidity—

or February ice—upon rising—her feet
on the floorboards—all stone and cloud.

Spoon, Fork, Plate

My spoons have disappeared. Trashed with yogurt
Cups, dumped with soggy cereal, where do they live?
The austere silverware drawer misses the plump curves.

Poon, a child bangs with her fist: *oon* is wind, or hurt,
Or a broguish *own.* She wants her baby spoon, heaves
The plastic substitute. Black ants scatter in droves.

In Anglo-Saxon, *spon* meant "chip," thin wood cut
With a concave swoop. Rich Venetians believed
"Apostle spoons" saved their children's lives:

St. Peter carved on the silver handle meant
Privilege and protection. Born with silvery
Spoons in their mouths, babies flung saints to the eaves.

My children lack manners, think the rules suck rotten eggs.
Erasmus of Rotterdam penned *On Civility in Children*
In 1530. Being a scholar of enlightenment and a humanist,

He thought children were people, and made their manners painless.
Moving on your chair creates the impression of breaking wind.
If you can't swallow food, turning and throwing it is best.

Turn away when spitting lest your saliva land on the hostess.
After wiping your nose, do not peer into it as if pearls were in
The handkerchief. Do not be afraid of vomiting if you must.

Like my children, the Roman upper class ate with three fingers, ring
And pinkie never soiled. In Tuscany, upper-class etiquette
Demanded a fork. Priests preached against the "little pitchforks."

Archbishop of Canterbury Thomas à Becket used the two-tine
Sort he'd found in Italy, considered effeminate
In stodgy Britain. Better for duels, the nobles thought.

While "Liberty, Equality, and Fraternity" rang in
The French Revolution, the wealthy—dying for refinement—
Upped the ante to four tines before the onslaught.

To have a fork of one's own, that aristocratic clang
Of one's metal on plate! Caution for the lowly: when asked to eat
From a common bowl, don't plunge hands before rank.

Near my spoonless silverware tray, an English Wedgwood bowl
Hides decaf tea bags and cane sugar. Its white neoclassical relief
Reminds me of everything I hated last summer in London.

The kings, queens, dukes, counts, dowagers, princesses, and earls.
The changing of guards and gold-rimmed china *ad nauseum,* the belief
In royal manners. Wedgwood himself liked the tea party in Boston.

Abolitionist and designer of coded upper-class dinnerware,
He made antislavery cameos of a man in chains, whose motif
Read, "Am I not a man and a brother?" A gift for his grandson, Charles Darwin.

Kraków Blues

Not the Duke and not Bessie, not Nina or Charlie,
in sulfur-dense, humid wafts off the Vistula;
a boy maybe, a girl, wandering the Rynek,
cobblestone alleys, past striped umbrella tables,
clotted with Czechs and Hungarians,
into the bare-shelved food shops, nodding
to the butcher with his one side of stringy beef,
an old man maybe, white-haired and dumbfounded
as he reads *We shall overcome* in the Polish daily,
sees pictures of African Americans in food lines;
a raven-haired aunt maybe, in heels
that clack on the stones, out for scarce
tins of mackerel and jars of pickled herring,
mussed from cooking, her white sleeve singed
at the cuff; not Billie in one-down love,
or James doing the Funky Chicken, not so tangible really
as a wail or a swagger or a down-and-dirty tub,
a twenty-year-old off soon to the army,
college kids organizing for the shipyard workers
(another killed by police in a stairwell);
a young woman who smuggles fur coats
from Russia, reading Hemingway on a bench;
hubbub of summer tourists in the market, free
to buy and leave, mispronouncing the three words
they've learned, but proud, friendly, eager
to barter for bright woolen shawls; a young poet
maybe, or a musician, hard to know—filling erasures
of history and self with down-under syncopated
Tin Pan Alley riffs in the coffeehouse where lyrics
are tickets for trains pulsing on tracks no one can see.

Counterpoint

1.

I wish I could jazz forth a trumpet from my pocket,
A sax from my belly, a clarinet from my larynx.
My music lessons short-circuited in the third grade.
Beware the child who speaks without words, who sidles
Up to a piano as if it were human and plays for days
In a shroud of harmonic occlusion, neither naive, nor aware
Her inner life's a shrine the jealous will invade.

2.

Ah, she's in there walloping Mozart again, mastering
The art of practice. At least Beethoven couldn't have heard
Himself parodied. Gifted fingers and ear unite to outsmart
The score. The money, the time, the nagging and bickering—

Then I hear it, the long Chopin cadenza like the flourish
And pitch of a cardinal darting from our driveway at dusk.

3.

Word-free is my anchorless boat, spinning lopsided
Down a river studded with dragonflies. In a staccato
Run to the sea, the river erases what I thought was thought.

September 11

after George Herbert

Understanding something isn't prayer, necessarily.

Cinnamon croissants, hot pretzels speared under glass,
café latte behind hostility's headlines. God

in the details: man well-dressed, reversed thunder
from a milky-breathed baby. Engines pitted against

time, takeoff code from the air traffic control tower,
radar plumbing the atmosphere. Slumped in blue jean

bell-bottoms, teens nodding to heavy metal on ear phones.
Hard not to hear. Journey of strangers locked in a tube.

Annals of the absurd faithful, prepared to meet the stars
in a biff of pressured air. Softness of cruising, bliss

of landing, love waiting in the wings, the cockpit.
In ordinary hearts, a slivered wish. Muted joy

at unfastening seatbelts. Paraphrased as relief.
Flying from ice pole to desert to birders' paradise

in privileged pilgrimage, the best cuts of wool.
Storing luggage in overheads, not knowing

the six days world would be transposed in one hour

Slave Huts, Bonaire

Maker, modeler, bearer, begetter
   In copses of oleander, in cactus shade,

Among squid, flounder, sea cucumber, coral,
   They mar the sea, the white sand.

On a slender shore, mud huts the size
   Of my daughter's playhouse

With doors at waist level and one window
   Housed five African men on the floor

After they harvested salt by hand all day
   In evaporation salt pans, free Saturday nights

To walk barefoot seven hours to Rincón
   In the green hills, then back by Monday.

The obelisks signaled, *Drop them off here,*
   As Dutch traders sipped rum on the deck.

Maker, modeler, bearer, begetter
   Four flamingos perch one-legged

In an irrigation ditch, as trade winds
   Lift white wisps from the salt mountains.

A Toyota scurries by to catch the sunset at Pink Beach.
   The company cranes are hauled up for the night.

Maker, modeler, bearer, begetter
   This is who we are, whom you created.

Pure Music

Tonight I am trying to listen, to do nothing but hear the leaves, their green wind
   chime.
In the random rustle of air, I hear a beckoning.

Where will I go if I follow? The hold I have is slender, without branches or roots.
The music of the universe is no comfort. In the leaves I hear my breath quickening.

In a cellar ten years ago my friend hanged herself while her husband slept upstairs.
She left a shrine of letters at her feet, one of them mine, complaint disguised as
   apology.

If I try to imagine her rapid gasps, I can. To empty the mind is to be less attached.
In the leaves I hear a flute. I want—

Let your breath slow down, let it make a wind tunnel in your throat. Maybe I don't
   exist
the way others do. When I call to myself, when I let go—

In despair, Moses waited in the cleft of the mountain. He heard God pass by.
What sound could that have been?

Sycamore leaves fall last. Tight-fisted when snow comes early, they claw the
   ground.
Who could have known she'd make a noose for herself?

Air, breath, and spirit share one word in Hebrew. It's said spirit does not need
   breath
to be alive. Is there intention in the wind chime, or is it the music of nothing?

Oasis

Not a watering hole with trees, but a pit dug
In the sand. A place no one else would notice.

No camels, or tents. No umbrellas tilted against the sun.
Dune mirage for protection. Risk of being buried alive.

Call that a desert of desire, if you choose. Or the wanderer's
Arid heart. Let your armies battle till Doomsday to find it.

I can find it even by starlight. If I dig deep enough,
Night winds do not graze my forehead.

I can pillow myself in the stillness. The heat
Of my body is no stranger to the heat of the sand.

In a grain of sand I can uncover a prism by which
To approach mystery. Even as we speak, women

In ancient villages scoop sand from their doorsills.
Deserts expand, change shape. A pit the size of a small body

Can't give shelter forever. There's no need to remind me of that.
My oasis persists the way a myth harbors what is true.

Habits

1.

Long melancholy thread, muslin wisp that binds,
garment handed down from generation to generation,
ticking frayed, buttons cracked, sailor collar stained,

worn by each child in the third year, in spring,
when tulips in the large white pitcher by the window
distill the scent of rain and wet mulch—

worn and tattered, washed and starched, pressed
into service by hands that once thrust out
of its sleeves like the balled rags of a scarecrow,

coat of many colors, here in the black trunk I open,
strewn across my younger daughter's plastic rain jacket.
She waits by the door in red rubber boots,

howling to be let outside, away from my watchful eye—

2.

She has a habit, we say, meaning it has her,
riding habit, clerical habit, habit of speech, force of habit inhabiting her—
The Surgeon General is wrong. Veins so thin, purple anemones

bloomed from wrist to elbow, the oxygen mask chafed her cheeks.
Time to prepare, not time enough to stop time. One half-moon
eye in blue shallows watched me watch it close. Oh, help me,

I don't know what to call this evasion. *Life is sad,* she whispered,
observing my grief, *you have to have SOME pleasure.* My daughter
stomps her feet on the mesh rug, bangs the door, until I slip

the stiff noisy jacket over her shoulders, angle her thin arms in.
Caught in the mirror she turns, her tears rainbow the sun,
her face my mother's face, lifted toward mine.

3.

The crocuses, plump and maroon as plums, have poked
through a thicket of wet leaves, a mound of pebbled rot
where snowdrops hang their heads like monks at prayer.

I untangle the hose, a frozen figure eight, stick my fingers
two inches into the sawdust on the yellow fence, slap
topsoil on the exposed roots of the Peace rose in the courtyard.

I sang, I kept singing, stables and angels and ladders,
and the numbers kept rising on the green monitor, lifting her
to sentience for a brief moment of recognition.

Brave, she said, *I feel brave,* and I invented verses to keep
the music going, to keep her fingers tight on mine, past the time
her eye closed, into the silence and the space beyond.

4.

My mother's ashes in a box on a shelf with other numbered
boxes, her name printed on a tag.
Rubble. Split sidewalk. A sculptor's shattered mold.

Surely it couldn't be my mother's fractured wrist, calcium-
deficient hip. Not her deviated septum, waxy skull.
Not her breastbone vibrating below the oxygen mask.

I could have held her in my hands like rocks plucked
from cliffs, shards of what is irreducible,
what could still cut if I approached carelessly.

5.

I'm not inhaling, my mother would insist, tapping her cigarette
into the green ceramic ashtray. *But I am,* I'd say, *even my hair
inhales this stuff,* cracking the window open on the snow.

It's not too late. But thick heart, thin tubes, lungs like wet sponge,
desire in the suck, the root, bald head in the womb wall.
After the funeral, my daughters scoop maple seeds into their pockets,

wing the withered ones off the stone fence. I can hear her making coffee,
anxious it won't be ready on time. The gas flame fans the burner,
water hisses in the pot. She's at the window again, choking on phlegm.

6.

I opened the box, pulled out the plastic bag, red garbage
tie twisted twice. Inside a rectangular label: October 19, 1996.
Not shards or rocks, but bonemeal. I took it to the scale:

four and three-quarter pounds. Enough to fertilize the memorial
trees we'll plant next month. *As the days of a tree
are the days of my people.* Wasp trees, ant trees, rat trees,

fat trees (kapok, the pillow stuffer, the Cuban belly palm),
so shall the seed be sown. The exfoliating bark of the *Stewartia*
is the wound it grows by. It flowers late, after the intoxicating lilt

of cherry and pear, after the spring rains. Agency of forgetting,
the rain. Agency of accident, of reconstruction.
I cannot watch again. I will not water the pitted

ground with my prayers, or spend nights in the garden
singing to the god of drought. Have you watched a tree die?
Pathetic fisted leaves, cocoons like burial shrouds.

How much should I save, one pound, or two?

First Laws

Every body continues in its state of rest, but tonight I have
to tell you we have divided yours into two principalities:
domain of black box on the linen closet's top shelf—

out of reach of overzealous cleaners, myself included,
who might discard you without thinking, or
grandchildren who might dump you into teacups—

and domain of nature, fistfuls of ash tucked into humus
and peat moss in pits dug in the yard, fertilizing the roots
of two white dogwoods and a pale cream sapling,

matter which cannot (remember, cannot) be destroyed. Each at rest
continuing, *or of uniform motion in a straight line,* straight through
the summer when drought turned the leaves to cylinders,

when Dad began screaming that the trees were dying, why
couldn't I do anything. I hung a thimble of ash from a dead branch,
soaked the roots. A body in linear movement *unless it is compelled to change*

that state by forces impressed upon it. And what could have pressed
you, Mother, if love did not? "I just want one more cigarette before I die,"
you begged from under your oxygen mask. "Take me to the back porch."

To every action force there is an equal and opposite reaction force,
and so breath is its own resistance, its own memorial. My opposite,
my appositive. My pleas to quit. The pen presses back against my hand.

Elsewhere

after "Looking for Poetry"

I came here so I might not feel sunlight on my face.
Carlos Drummond de Andrade searched for the key by not

Looking—a cavern opening to a waterfall, prisms of syllable-
Music. What I crave is molten, made by the untamable.

Carlos, we must talk. I've begun to sing the secrets of houses.
My mazurka, my yacht, my diamond shoe. My sea's noise.

Scrutiny is a faucet dripping despite pliers,
The globes form perfectly in sequence, hypnotic prayer

To the angel of reason. I can't make a wheelbarrow
Depend upon the dirt that fills it. You would say what broke

Wasn't crystal. I broke my mother's only crystal bowl
After supper, hands too small for that weight.

I knew, even then, what cannot be held without risk.
Oh, you'll call on me tomorrow if the storm surge

Doesn't wash away the bridge tonight. I can't look
At the tides, never mind study them. I search for nothing.

The New Creation

And then there was the nothing that is something else,
we saw what was created and could not be entirely

displeased. It was good in its way, morphine drip
unhooked, blood bags and oxygen removed.

In the beginning, we had not wanted this night.
Earth was enough. Oh, stubborn matter

that we were, lichen clinging to rocks, worms snug
in wormholes. We loved the firmament too much,

rivers and valleys, birds and beasts and our image
in the likeness, our dominion over every creeping thing.

Did we misunderstand the gift? Who said we should
just let her go, let her drift off as we watched,

down an uncharted river, and call it good, pronounce
it a blessing from God? This much at first, absence of pain.

And then, day returning to day, night to night,
a terrible peace descending on the plains

as the storm edged across the mountain clefts, hurling
its lightning elsewhere, and we were alone.

Aria

After the funeral, a bird—
frantic or ecstatic or gone mad
in the rhododendron thickets—
hammered open my night,
full of verve,
sure of his pitch,
the sweltering room
levitated in miracle
and good news.

Then swift and deafening,
a spring downpour
silenced him.

When Invisible Is an Invitation

In the spring of my disappearance
   Pear trees shed white blossoms
      As usual on my narrow street

Pregnant with light, they lighten
   The footsteps of my elderly neighbor
      On his noon walk to the mailbox

Licked envelopes drop
      Into the well of uncertainty

How do I know?—
      Spring has always annoyed me

I hear the dog walkers frisking like pups
   In the field across the street—
      They love their hostile mutt
        They love to do X and Y in bed

I live in a cave with a paper opening—

I'm learning the art of disappearing
   Involves someone who doesn't notice you're gone

And when it's done?—
      Shade in all the windows, except

The cracked one painted white

Dwell

And I shall dwell in the house of the Lord forever
Psalm 23

But is there clutter in the house of the Lord,
stacks of unanswered prayers on the desk,

for instance, or white terry cloth robes dangling
from doorknobs, their belt tips soiled black,

or gobs of angel hair gumming up the pipes
as sticky CDs skip through the morning cantatas,

or an infidel army of dust mites pillaging cushions
on the velvet throne—

I would want to know these things before I agreed
to move. Cleanliness ranks with godliness,

I've been told, and clutter's a curse on one's house.
One can't see into the heart of a clutterer,

who knows what lurks in the leaky valves
or flooded chambers,

tattered flaps and pock-marked walls. In a mess
like that, love can get trashed.

I'd better put my own house in order. Why not
start with *dwell* and dust the hell out of it?

Somewhere, a Nest

Birds line their nests with herbs to kill bacteria.

Birds weave scat into their nests to scare off predators.

What we can't do with hands birds do with beaks,
weaving a home in hours on someone else's branch.

I have always loathed the *whoo* of mourning doves.

Birds can plan ahead, anticipate where
twigs are hidden by the research team.

Mourning doves know too much.

Birds can love an empty egg.

Who can love emptiness enough to sit on it?

Birds inhabit our tottering babels; just one wind.

Messengers of the Greek gods, birds didn't shit on shoulders or swords.

That dart, rustle, and swoop, that wholly other.

"Dwell Nowhere and Bring Forth the Mind"

Diamond Sutra

But I'm most afraid of nowhere. The vortex of crows
when abruptly they rouse off the ground. That kind

of crying. House without walls. Speckle in the black
expanse that didn't become a star. The sutra instructs

To dwell with color is to risk—
But I've worked hard to learn the simplest earthly

lessons. Snowdrops breaking ice in the garden.
A tint of lavender in the Russian sage blooming against

my yellow fence. Blackberry in my tea, ochre brine
on the cup. Perhaps to dwell *somewhere* for now.

This hunter green bed and *this* white oak table.
There's not enough time—

A Bristle of Wings in the Ivy

When the gong sounded, I was alone in the stone tower—
A bristle of wings in the ivy, dry-necked mortar in the walls.

I sat like a monk at prayer. Wind whistled through the cracks
And I heard you call me:

>Come back to your simple

>Table, your garden of burgundy lilies, that chair in the corner
>Where you can see chickadees on the feeder chased off

>By squirrels. We can give you solitude. Soup. We can bring
>The moon to you by cutting a branch from the sycamore.

>We hurt you because we are human. We couldn't
>Hear your voice in a hurricane's silence.

Then I called to you:

>You haven't wronged me. I've needed to live as I have,
>With *suppose* as the friend I turn to.

>I haven't loved you deeply enough.
>The mockingbird in the ivy could not steal my song otherwise.

The bird left me. The gong was gone. I opened my door to the wild stairs.